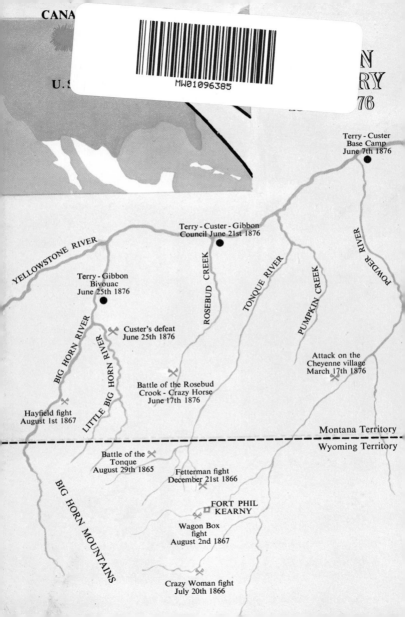

CANA...

U.S...

...N...RY
...76

Terry - Custer
Base Camp
June 7th 1876

YELLOWSTONE RIVER

Terry - Custer - Gibbon
Council June 21st 1876

POWDER RIVER

ROSEBUD CREEK

TONGUE RIVER

PUMPKIN CREEK

Terry - Gibbon
Bivouac
June 25th 1876

BIG HORN RIVER

Custer's defeat
June 25th 1876

LITTLE BIG HORN RIVER

Battle of the Rosebud
Crook - Crazy Horse
June 17th 1876

Attack on the
Cheyenne village
March 17th 1876

Hayfield fight
August 1st 1867

Montana Territory
Wyoming Territory

Battle of the
Tongue
August 29th 1865

Fetterman fight
December 21st 1866

BIG HORN MOUNTAINS

FORT PHIL
KEARNY

Wagon Box
fight
August 2nd 1867

Crazy Woman fight
July 20th 1866

The Battle of the Little Big Horn

CUSTER'S LAST STAND

written and illustrated
by FRANK HUMPHRIS

Ladybird Books Loughborough

Introduction

The most sensational battle in the long history of warfare between the soldiers of the United States and the American Indians took place on June 25th 1876.

Imagine yourself as a trooper in the United States Cavalry, riding towards the valley of the Little Big Horn on that June morning. For the last forty days you have been in the saddle, travelling about thirty miles a day. Your heavy army issue shirt and thick flannel lined blue jacket are caked with sweat and dust. Around your waist, the long-barrelled Colt revolver and twenty four rounds of ammunition seem to get heavier and heavier; as the single-shot Springfield carbine bumps against your leg, you thank your lucky stars that the sabres were left behind. You also have with you a water bottle with, at best, luke-warm water, a hundred cartridges for the carbine, some rations and camp utensils in the saddle bags, a blanket roll and a twelve pound bag of oats for the horse.

4

At the head of the column, a lithe figure in fringed buckskin coat and wide brimmed hat calls his officers together and tells them the scouts have reported a large Indian village some fifteen miles away in the valley of the Little Big Horn.

The order is given to advance – and so Lieutenant-Colonel (brevet Major General) George Armstrong Custer leads his 7th Cavalry on to meet the Indians – and destiny.

An uneasy peace had existed in the lands of the Teton (or western branch of the Sioux nation) since Red Cloud's war ended with the treaty of 1868.

This treaty, made between the United States Government and the Indians, solemnly promised that all the Powder River country, which included the Black Hills of Dakota, would belong to the Indians '. . . as long as the grass shall grow.'

Red Cloud and his followers, and Spotted Tail, the Brulé Sioux chief, were now living on reservations following their visit to Washington, where, perhaps for the first time, the chiefs realised the might and power of the white man.

But there were still many Indians who scorned the example of Red Cloud and Spotted Tail and refused to give up their freedom.

New leaders had arisen who were determined to fight for their land and the right to live as they had always lived. Prominent among the Sioux were the Hunkpapa chief, Sitting Bull, the great warriors Crazy Horse, Gall, Hump, and Rain in the Face. Allied to them were those famous fighters, the northern Cheyennes.

Then, in 1874, the Government sent a Survey Expedition – ironically led by Lieutenant-Colonel George A. Custer – to the Black Hills. And the expedition found . . . GOLD! This discovery was to shatter any hopes there may have been for a permanent peace treaty.

When the discovery of gold was made known, the newspapers went wild. 'Gold from the grass roots down!' ran the headlines.

The news let loose a rush of prospectors to Sioux territory and over once quiet pony trails moved horsemen, freight wagons and mule trains with camping and mining gear. They poured in from all over the country.

The Sioux viewed this invasion of their land with anger and alarm.

Yet another treaty was being broken – the treaty which stated that: 'No white person or persons shall be permitted to settle upon or occupy any portion of Indian territory, or, without the consent of the Indians first had and obtained, to pass through the same.'

Once again the white man's words were hollow.

The passage of so many people drove the game far away from the neighbourhood of the trails. With parties of white men roaming the hunting grounds, even the Indians' food supply was threatened.

Within a short space of time the town of Deadwood and a score of other mining camps sprang up in the Black Hills. With the miners and prospectors came other fortune hunters – saloon keepers, gamblers, thieves and gunmen and other riff-raff of the frontier.

Deadwood, South Dakota 1876

9

Having started the trouble, the Government now attempted to halt the rush of white men into Indian country by sending troops to round up the trespassers, and turn back those who were on their way. But it was a half-hearted effort. Those miners who were caught and arrested were promptly released from custody by the civil courts. All the time hundreds of others bypassed the army patrols, spurred on by rumours of new 'strikes'.

The Sioux were violently angry.

Seeing the soldiers' efforts were having little or no effect, they went on the warpath and attacked the white men whenever they could.

Ambushes were laid. Men prospecting on lonely creeks were caught and killed. Stage coaches were attacked. Smaller trains of three or four wagons were destroyed, the occupants left dead and dying beside their burnt-out vehicles.

There was an immediate – and familiar – outcry: 'What was the army doing to protect the citizens against these savages?'

Fifteen hundred miles away in Washington, the government had difficult decisions to make – political decisions. If force was used to remove the gold seekers it would be an unpopular move with the general public – who were the voters – most of whom had little sympathy with the Indians in any case. If the miners were left in the Black Hills the treaty would be finished.

It was evident that the army's attempt to clear the Black Hills of gold seekers was doomed to failure. There were just too many, the troops were too few and the country too vast.

Faced with this impossible situation the government sent out a Commission to try to buy the Black Hills from the Indians. But the Sioux were in a sullen and angry mood. To them, Paha Sapa, the Black Hills, were sacred medicine ground.

Large numbers of Indians gathered at the council. There were arguments and a good deal of hostility, although some of the reservation Indians, knowing the futility of resistance and having some idea of the value of money, demanded sums from twenty million to seventy million dollars.

The government's offer of six million dollars was treated with contempt.

The non-reservation Indians refused to consider any price. Crazy Horse scornfully observed, 'One does not sell the earth on which the people walk.'

The Commission returned having accomplished nothing.

Events were rapidly reaching a stage where war was inevitable. In December 1875, an order was issued that ALL Indians were to come in to the reservations by January 31st 1876 or be classed as 'hostiles'. Those who remained out would be brought in by force.

It would have been difficult to obey even if the Indians were willing, for it was midwinter and travelling in the deep snow would have been a severe hardship. Some of the messengers sent out by the authorities found themselves 'snowed in' and unable to return.

The deadline passed.

Thus the stage was set for the military authorities to take action.

Snow still covered the ground when the first blow fell on the Cheyenne village of Two Moon. A shouted alarm roused the sleeping Indians as, in the freezing cold of early morning, the soldiers charged into the village. The startled warriors just had time to grab weapons and help the women and children escape up the nearby slopes before the village was captured and set on fire.

With horrified anger the Cheyennes watched their homes and all their food supplies and clothing go up in smoke.

And afterwards?

With only the clothes they stood up in, they trudged for three days until a friendly Sioux village was reached. If they were not hostile before, they certainly were now!

The campaign of 1876

The attack on the Indian village was the beginning of the campaign of 1876. It was part of the army plan to strike into hostile territory from three directions.

Imagine a triangle standing on one point. At the top left point was Colonel Gibbon's force marching east. From the top right point General Alfred H. Terry's command marched to the west. From the bottom point General Crook's command moved north.

The Indians were somewhere in the middle of the triangle. Early in June the forces of Terry and Gibbon met at the Yellowstone River, and on June 21st the officers went aboard the supply steamer *Far West* to map out the next move. In the meantime Major Reno reported finding a trail that showed that a large body of Indians were moving towards the Big Horn region.

Terry decided to move in that direction.

Custer and the 7th Cavalry, which formed part of Terry's command, were instructed to find and follow the Indian trail while the Terry-Gibbon forces moved further west to the Big Horn valley. By timed marches, the two columns planned to be in position by June 26th, to close in and trap the Indians between them.

As the 7th rode away, Custer's senior officers wished him luck. 'Now Custer, don't be greedy, wait for us,' Gibbon remarked. 'No, I won't,' said Custer – a reply which could be taken either way.

Terry, Custer and Gibbon aboard the Far West

George Armstrong Custer commanding the 7th Cavalry was a flamboyant and controversial officer. During the Civil War his outstanding courage and leadership gained him rapid promotion to the brevet rank of major general when only twenty five years of age. The 'boy General', as he was called, was a popular hero. He had long fair hair, and wore a distinctive uniform of his own design with a wide sailor collar and flowing red tie.

After the war he reverted to his regular army rank of captain and by 1876 was a lieutenant-colonel. He has been glamorised as a famous Indian fighter.

However, with the exception of the 'battle' of the Washita when, in a surprise attack he destroyed the village of Black Kettle and took many prisoners, his Indian fighting experiences were limited to skirmishes of a minor nature.

Major Marcus Reno also had a distinguished career in the Civil War but his conduct at the Little Big Horn was greatly criticised. He survived the battle, but it ruined his career.

Among the other officers was Captain Tom Custer, the Colonel's brother; Captain Myles Keogh, who was formerly in the Papal Guard in Rome, and Captain Frederick Benteen who, following the battle of the Washita, was highly critical of his commanding officer.

Lieutenant
W W Cooke
*Adjutant of
the 7th Cavalry*

Capt.
Tom
Custer

Capt.
Myles Keogh
Formerly of the Papal Guard

Major
Marcus Reno
*He survived the
battle but his
career was ruined*

Capt.
Frederick Benteen
A strong critic of Custer

Custer's command consisted of 617 officers and men, 33 Arikara Indian scouts and some 20 civilians. These included a brother, Boston Custer, a nephew, a news correspondent, mule packers and six Crow scouts who possessed a knowledge of the region.

He refused the offer of three Gatling guns (and what a difference those machine guns spitting up to a thousand shots a minute would have made) and also declined a further four troops of the 2nd Cavalry, being confident that the 7th could handle any number of Sioux and Cheyenne they might meet.

In Custer's pocket were written instructions to follow the Indian trail only as far as the Little Big Horn valley, not into it; then wait to link up with Gibbon on June 26th for a joint attack. This was the important part of the plan – the part that Custer did not carry out and which contributed to the final disaster. Whether Custer wilfully disobeyed, or whether the orders gave him sufficient latitude to act independently, is debatable.

For three days the regiment followed the wide trail of an Indian village on the march. Custer, believing he would find about a thousand or fifteen hundred Indians, was determined to pursue until he found them.

At one point the column was only a day's ride from where General Crook's force had fought a big battle with the Sioux and Cheyennes a week previously. Unable to defeat the Indians, Crook had withdrawn but all this was completely unknown to Custer – or to General Terry.

A night march on June 24th brought the regiment close to the divide separating the valleys of the Rosebud and Little Big Horn rivers. The following morning Custer rode to the crest of the hills, where the Crow scouts pointed to the haze in a distant valley.

'Many Indians – great village,' they warned him. But even with field glasses Custer failed to see what the keen eyes of the scouts saw, and still had no definite knowledge of the exact location of the Indians, or their numbers.

The commander rejoined the main column and then learned that Indians had been sighted on the back trail. There was no longer any hope of surprise. It was possibly at this point that Custer made his fatal decision to attack. Convinced the enemy now knew of the soldiers' arrival and might escape before the link-up with Terry and Gibbon could be made, he gave orders for the advance.

The regiment was divided into four columns. Captain Benteen with three companies was sent to scout the hills to the south-west. Major Reno with three companies continued down to the valley with instructions – 'to charge the Indians wherever you find them and you will be supported by the whole outfit.'

Custer, with five companies, remained with Reno for some distance, then turned right and followed the line of hills leading to the lower end of the village. The remaining company was left to follow Custer and Reno with the slower moving pack mules.

The first encounter

Major Reno's three companies covered the distance down to the Little Big Horn at a fast trot and crossed to the west bank of the river.

Here the companies formed into battle line and advanced along the valley towards the great encampment some three miles away.

Ahead of them a rising cloud of dust thickened; as the soldiers drew near they could see it was kicked up by the ponies of hundreds of warriors between them and the village.

Never had the troopers seen such numbers of Indians as now rode towards them, yelling and whooping.

Rifles began to flash. Two troop horses became un-
manageable and bolted, carrying their riders in amongst
the Indians. The two were never seen again.

Reno was faced with a difficult decision. Should he
try to charge through the massed warriors, or adopt a
defensive position and wait for Custer and his promised
support?

The major flung up his arm and ordered his men to
dismount and fight on foot. A volley roared out from the
firing line checking the Indians, but at that moment the
army's Arikara scouts on the left gave way. The troops
were forced to move back to a small wood to avoid
being outflanked.

Step by step, firing all the time, the thin line of troopers retreated to the shelter of the timber, but here too, the Indians were gradually closing in. Bullets ripped through the foliage, hit trees and whined off at a vicious angle. Here and there men fell. Shots began to come from the rear where the Indians were trying to get at the horses.

With the Sioux now on three sides, Reno decided to break out of the wood, charge through the encircling warriors and make for the high ground across the river.

Unfortunately, in the uproar and general confusion, the order could not be heard by everyone. Some troopers only realised a move was being made when they saw their comrades mounting – and several men were left behind.

Reno galloped out of the timber followed by the disorganised column and the retreat became a rout with the Sioux racing alongside, shooting and charging into the troopers, dragging the stragglers and wounded from their saddles.

But there were deeds of heroism too. Young Lieutenant Benny Hodgson's leg was shattered by the bullet which killed his horse. A trooper reined in and helped him to cross the river, where a second bullet ended his life. The famous scout Charlie Reynolds fought to the last in the timber and was killed as he rode out. Many another fell in that mad scramble across the river.

Respite and reinforcements

The survivors reached the bluffs exhausted and dangerously low in ammunition. Casualties had been heavy. Three officers and thirty two troopers dead, seven wounded and nineteen missing from a total of one hundred and twelve men. Some of the missing managed to escape and rejoin their comrades later. Once on the hilltop the troopers fought back, but even here they were under murderous fire from nearby heights that the Indians had occupied.

Just after four o'clock in the afternoon Captain Benteen's column, returning from its scout to the south west, joined Reno's men on the hill. It was with enormous relief Reno received these reinforcements.

As the troopers joined the defence line the enemy fire died down, and large numbers of Indians were seen galloping towards the north.

Shortly after came the sound of heavy firing from far down the valley. Custer was in action at last!

The pack mules with the ammunition having at last arrived, the other officers now urged Major Reno to move in support of Custer. Reluctantly he agreed, and carrying the wounded in blankets the column moved off. They did not get far before furious Indian attacks drove them back to the hilltop, where they dug in as best they could. All the rest of the day they fought for their lives.

Reno's small command had faced the full power of the Sioux and Cheyennes, and had been hurled back.

CRAZY HORSE
(Tashunka Witko)
War Chief of the
Ogalalla Sioux
Taken from a photo said to be
Crazy Horse. No completely
authentic likeness exists.

SITTING BULL
(Tatanka iyo'take)
Chief and Medicine Man of the Hunkpapa Sioux.
Accepted as the most important Chief at the Little Big Horn.

The Indian Chiefs

Custer, hurrying down river to strike the village from the other end was still unaware of the great numbers opposed to him. It was probably the largest gathering of Indians ever known on the Plains.

The Sioux tribes were there in force – Hunkpapas, Minneconjous, Blackfeet Sioux, Sans Arcs, Brulés and Ogalallas. Across one of the small creeks were the fighting Cheyennes. A number of Arapahoes and hostiles from other tribes were in the camps. In all, over twelve thousand people with possibly three or four thousand warriors.

All the chiefs of the various tribes met as equals, but

RAIN IN THE
FACE
(I tó o ma ga ju)
Sioux Warrior
Said to have killed
Tom Custer

GALL *(Pizi)*
War Chief of the Hunkpapa Sioux

TWO MOON
(Ish i ēyo nis si)
Cheyenne Chief

one stood out and was acknowledged as the most important chief. This was Sitting Bull.

He has often been pictured as a cruel and cunning savage, particularly after the shock of Custer's defeat, but there is no evidence for this. On the contrary, he could be friendly towards individual white men; but he was a patriot, fighting for his country and angry at the injustices done to his race.

He was also an astute and capable politician – in modern times he would have made a notable nationalist leader. It was his organising ability that kept the tribes together for the struggle he knew must come.

Confident in their great strength, the Indians awaited the bluecoats.

After separating from Reno, Custer led the way up the slopes at a sharp pace, keeping below the crest of the hills which hid him from the Indians' view.

Some distance had been covered when he halted the command and rode up to the ridge to look down into the valley. For the first time he saw the great Indian village spread out below him.

According to orderly trumpeter John Martin who was with him, the General surveyed the scene, turned to his companions and exclaimed, 'We've got them. We've caught them napping. Come on!' Martin was then ordered back to find Benteen and deliver an urgent message. The message read, 'Benteen. Come on. Big village. Be quick. Bring packs. P.S. Bring pacs.'

Martin turned his horse and rode away. He was the last white man to see Custer and his men alive.

Down in the village the alarm was spreading. Although the Indians knew the soldiers were coming, the actual attack took them by surprise and there was great excitement and confusion. Frantic mothers grabbed their babies; women, children and the old hurried to escape; warriors raced to catch their horses.

It may have been this initial confusion that led Custer to believe the Indians were running away, and accounted for his first exultant exclamation.

Several Indians later admitted that they *were* caught napping and knew nothing of the attack until they heard the gunfire. Then it was a rush to arm themselves and get ready for the fight.

Preparing for battle

It was Indian practice to prepare carefully before going into battle; some wore special war shirts and head-dresses or relied on the protective powers of symbolic 'medicine' and war paint. Others preferred to fight stripped down to breech cloth and moccasins.

One young Cheyenne gave a detailed description of his war dress which is particularly interesting as it shows the importance attached to symbolic items. This preparation was for the battle with General Crook's force which took place a week before the Little Big Horn.

On that occasion his body was painted with yellow earth paint; then his father tied the stuffed skin of a king-fisher to his son's scalplock because . . . 'the kingfisher never misses its prey!' In the bird's beak were red feathers to represent the flash from a gun. A whistle made from an eagle's wing bone was hung round the warrior's neck. When this was blown the enemy bullets would cause no harm. A kingfisher symbol was painted on the horse's flank to give it direction, and lastly, 'medicine' dust was blown on the horse's hooves to give them speed and lightness.

At the Little Big Horn there was no time for such elaboration, though doubtless many warriors stopped the few extra seconds to don at least part of their war paint and costume.

Man and horse in full war paint and ready for battle.

When Reno began the attack, the three cavalry detachments were completely out of touch with each other. Reno thought Custer was following up to give support, but Custer had left the trail and struck off across the hills. By the time Reno was in action, Custer was at least one, perhaps two, miles away behind the bluffs on the other side of the river.

Benteen, having scouted miles to the south without result, had returned to the trail when Martin rode up with Custer's message urging him to 'come on' etc. Benteen hurried on to find Custer, but found Reno instead and went to the aid of the battered survivors on the hill-top.

Custer's exact route is uncertain, but approximately four miles downriver from where he had left Reno, the column emerged from the hills and turned towards the river roughly opposite the centre of the great encampment.

According to one version, only a few warriors were left in that area, most of them being at the upper end of the valley fighting Reno. But as soon as the soldiers were seen, four brave Cheyennes – Bobtail Horse, Roan Bear, Buffalo Calf and one whose name is not known – crossed the river, concealed themselves in a gully, and opened fire at the approaching column.

Not knowing how many were facing him, Custer became cautious and called a halt to probe the strength of the opposition. The delay was fatal.

On the defensive

Any account of the final struggle can only be conjecture, based on information given by the Indians at a much later date, and the mute evidence of the stricken battlefield as seen two days after the battle. Unfortunately the Indian accounts vary so widely it is impossible to reconcile them. The version already recounted has Custer halted by a few Cheyennes; another version says the soldiers actually reached the river; in yet another that they were halted some distance back on the hill.

Whichever is accepted there is no doubt that Custer was quickly forced on the defensive by overwhelming numbers.

When word reached the Indians facing Reno that more blue-coats were at the other end of the village, war chief Gall raced back to take charge of the main Indian attack from the south. Followed by hundreds of excited warriors, he led the way up a dry coulée towards a ridge where Keogh's and Calhoun's two troops had dismounted to form a skirmish line.

The Sioux opened a heavy fire and by yelling and shouting soon succeeded in stampeding the horses. In this way the soldiers lost their reserve ammunition which was in the saddle bags. Then, as the troopers' fire grew less, out of the ravine poured a mass of yelling warriors. Calhoun's company was rushed and wiped out – the bronze horde crashed into and over Keogh's men and all was over in that part of the field.

Outnumbered and under fire from all sides, the three remaining companies were forced to retreat up the slope. Ravines and gullies cutting into the hill-side allowed the Indians to get in close. Every rock and bush concealed warriors increasingly well armed with guns and ammunition taken from the soldiers as they fell.

A brave Cheyenne chief, Lame White Man, led a sudden charge which cost him his life but shattered the Grey Horse Troop of Lieutenant Smith. All around men were dying. Captain Yates' troop was decimated – less than half of Tom Custer's remained.

Horses, wounded by bullet or arrow, reared and plunged away, adding to the chaos. Here and there a trooper dug frantically with a knife at a cartridge case jammed in his carbine.

Raked by fire from every direction, the remnants struggled to reach the crest of the hill with the hope of forming a defensive position on the top. They never reached it. Over the brow came Crazy Horse with his Ogalallas; Two Moon led the Cheyennes.

It was the final rush – a desperate hand to hand struggle – a confused, swirling, fighting mass as Custer and his comrades were overwhelmed. The General fell, shot through the temple and the left breast. A few yards away lay his brother, Tom. Captain Yates and Lieutenant Cooke, the adjutant with the luxurious side-whiskers, were nearby. Scattered around lay the bodies of the troopers who had rallied to the final stand.

The final desperate struggle

Four miles away on Reno's hill the fighting continued, until nightfall put an end to the gunfire and brought relief to the parched and weary defenders. Several more had been killed and wounded since the command returned from the disastrous attempt to reach Custer.

Dr Henry Porter, the only surviving surgeon, gained the lasting respect of the men he tended. Throughout the time on the bluffs he worked ceaselessly, ignoring the hostile bullets that thudded into the ground about the hollow where the wounded lay.

But the summer night was short.

At first light the shooting started again. Twice during the morning the soldiers were forced to launch counter attacks to drive the Indians back. Thirst became an agony, particularly to the wounded, and volunteers risked their lives under heavy fire to bring a few canteens of water from the river.

Then, late in the afternoon, the huge encampment was seen to be moving. Gradually the warriors withdrew from the bluffs and joined the great mass of Indians leaving the valley.

Counting the cost

Gibbon's troops, accompanied by General Terry, arrived at the valley the following morning. Some Crow scouts had already met the column with news of the defeat but the officers doubted the Indians' story. It was too incredible. Only when they reached the scene did the dreadful evidence of the tragedy that had befallen their comrades become evident.

The only living thing on the battlefield was Captain Keogh's horse, 'Comanche', so badly wounded that the Indians had left it behind.

Reno, Benteen and the other survivors on the hill-top were equally stunned when they met Terry and learned of the disaster. Although distant firing had been heard, it was assumed that Custer had been in a fight and had gone on to link up with Gibbon. No one dreamed that every man of the five troops had perished.

Of the six hundred officers and men of the 7th Cavalry who had ridden with the General to the Little Big Horn, less than half were left alive and fit for duty.

Besides Custer himself, his two brothers, a brother-in-law and a nephew died in the battle. Units from Gibbon's and Reno's forces gave what burial they could to the dead in the dusty, flinty ground and later markers were placed over the graves of those they were able to identify.

The total loss was two hundred and sixty two dead and fifty nine wounded, of whom seven died later.

Meanwhile the wounded men of Reno's command were transported in makeshift horse litters to the supply steamer *Far West* waiting at the junction of the Big and Little Horn rivers. It was an agonising, painful journey of many miles over rough trails to reach the boat. Steaming day and night, the *Far West* reached Fort Lincoln on 5th July when the wounded were transferred to the post hospital.

The news of the disaster came as a shock to the nation celebrating its first centenary, and aroused feelings of outraged anger against the Indians as the press recounted the goriest of stories about the mutilation of the fallen soldiers.

With the shock and horror came the questions.

How could an experienced soldier like Custer, with half his regiment, be wiped out by savages? Who was to blame? Whose the responsibility?

Inevitably there were those whose sympathies lay with the fallen hero, and Reno was accused of cowardice, first for abandoning the attack on the village, and secondly for failing to give Custer support when firing was heard down the valley. Others put the blame on Custer for disobeying Terry's orders, for dividing his forces, and for reckless overconfidence.

Still others insisted the cavalry had been led into a trap and called it a 'massacre'. The fact that the troops had sought out and attacked the Indians and not vice versa was ignored, and the desire for revenge was strong.

And what of the victorious Indians?

Ironically, the battle hastened the end of their freedom, for although it was their greatest victory, it was also their last. They had been attacked in the country that belonged to them but by defending themselves, they were considered to have violated the treaty which 'granted' them the right to live there in freedom.

From every quarter troops were marching into Sioux country searching for the various tribes, which, after leaving the Little Big Horn, had separated. This move to new hunting grounds was essential to replenish the meat and hides and buffalo robes necessary for the long winter months ahead.

The soldiers gave them no peace.

As the Indian villages were found, they were attacked and destroyed. With homes, food and clothing gone, those Indians that escaped wandered destitute and starving until even the hardiest were forced to submit.

Sitting Bull and his band escaped into Canada but, although treated fairly, they were an embarrassment to the Canadian Government. Eventually they, too, drifted back and surrendered.

For the Sioux and Cheyennes the old way of life was gone forever.

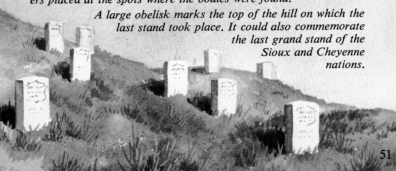

Today, the Custer Battlefield is a National Monument complete with museum where Indian and cavalry artifacts are exhibited. On the bluffs to the south-east the Reno-Benteen positions are also preserved. Custer's line of retreat can be traced by the stone markers placed at the spots where the bodies were found.

A large obelisk marks the top of the hill on which the last stand took place. It could also commemorate the last grand stand of the Sioux and Cheyenne nations.

MONUMENT
Lt. Col. Custer
Capt. T. Custer
Capt. Yates
Lt. Cooke
Lt. Smith
Lt. Reily

Lt. Crittenden
Capt. Keogh
Lt. Calhoun

Gall's attack

Crazy Horse's attack

Lame White Man's attack

BRULÉS

SANS ARCS

MINNECONJOUS

CHEYENNES

OGALALLAS

BLACKFEET SIOUX

HUNKPAPA

Indians attack

THE LITTLE BIG HORN
25th JUNE 1876